Living and Not Living

Living Things

This tree is **living**.

This tree is **not living**.

3

This duck is living.

This duck is not living.

This whale is living.

This whale is not living.

This flower is living.

This flower is not living.

This horse is living.

This horse is not living.

This kangaroo is living.

This kangaroo is not living.

This grass is living.

This grass is not living.

living

not living